Affirmations of the Fairy Cats

by Brenda June Saydak

Copyright © 2021 U.S. GAMES SYSTEMS, INC.
All rights reserved. The illustrations, cover design, and contents are protected by copyright. No part of this book may be reproduced in any form without permission in writing from the publisher, except by a reviewer who wishes to quote brief passages in connection with a review written for inclusion in a magazine, newspaper or website.

10 9 8 7 6 5 4 3 2 1

Made in China

Published by
U.S. GAMES SYSTEMS, INC.
179 Ludlow Street
Stamford, CT 06902 USA
www.usgamesinc.com

Table of Contents

Introduction 5
How to Use this Deck 7
The Cards 12
Inspiration 🍃 13
  Beauty 13
  Flight 15
  Fortitude 18
  Growth 20
  Metamorphosis 23
  Mystery 25
  Nurture 28
  Patterns 31
  Spring 34
  Stars 36

Contemplation ☾ 40
  Balance 40
  Courage 42
  Death 46
  Depth 49
  Environment 52
  Mindfulness 55
  Silence 58
  Solitude 62
  Sprout 65
  Winter 67

Comfort ♥ 71
- Adaptability 71
- Affection 73
- Autumn 76
- Faith 79
- Family 83
- Relaxation 85
- Scent 89
- Sleep 92
- Sun 95
- Tenacity 98

Celebration ★ 101
- Abundance 101
- Blossom 104
- Color 107
- Diversity 110
- Freedom 113
- Music 116
- Passion 119
- Summer 122
- Whimsy 125
- Wild 128

Bonus Card—Contentment 132

About the Artist and Author 136

Introduction

*Life is beautiful, magical, and
full of wonderment
I love my beautiful, magical,
wonderful life.*

Deep in the forest lies a hidden magical world just waiting for us to seek it out. It calls us away from all the mundane diversions of life with a tiny yet persistent voice in the back of our minds. Limitless joys await us if only we pay attention, and are willing to set out on a personal voyage of discovery. This is an intimate world best explored on one's own, but it's welcoming to all who heed its call. Here you will find an oasis of life-affirming tranquility, and a teacher of gentle life lessons. It asks us to see the world through a child's eyes once more, as an enticing place full of whimsy and limitless potential.

The forest is a great healer of mind, body and spirit, asking nothing of us but an open and receptive mind. This place provides an antidote to the harsh sounds, barren sights, and negative attitudes that modern life can bring. A walk in nature delights the eye, soothes the senses, and offers peace of mind and an opportunity to leave the trappings of civilization behind. It fills our soul with genuine and honest goodness, and allows us a quiet time to get to know ourselves better.

To help lighten the lessons contained in the cards, this forest is populated with the adorable fairy cats I've come to know over the past few years. With patience you'll come to see them too, if you learn to look with your heart as well as your eyes. Like house cats, these pretty kitty fairies, flying cat creatures and dainty feline unicorns live their lives with grace, self-confidence, and playfulness. In time, you'll begin to see them flitting about through the corner of your eye, and you'll begin to sense them peeking out at you between the leaves and flowers.

How To Use This Deck

This affirmations deck will help you foster a daily practice of positivity. The cards feature images of plants, flowers, and natural phenomena that remind us of the beauty of nature. The adorable kitties that live within this sanctuary ask us to suspend disbelief and open our hearts and minds to the possibility that magic still exists in our world. Some of the cards ask us to think deep about difficult messages, and these sweet creatures will gently guide you along the way. They'll help you see the world in a new light, sparking joy, creativity, self-confidence, and self-acceptance.

The deck consists of a bonus card and 40 cards divided into four sections, each with a distinct purpose. Inspiration cards offer us different ways to ignite creativity, with examples from nature to help encourage us to make positive changes in our lives. They remind us of the potential that is available to us, to create a life that expresses our authentic selves, and offers us the strength to get through difficult situations.

Contemplation cards help us deal with the more difficult aspects of life, like fear. They share suggestions on how to work through problems when you're feeling overwhelmed. These cards offer insights to help develop coping skills and ways to see difficult times as periods of growth and potential. Comfort cards reassure us when times are dark, and offer reminders of the many ways that others in our lives can support us when we need it. They ask us to take time for self-care, and to remember to make our own needs a priority. Celebration cards remind us of how abundant our lives are, and ask us to be always thankful. They offer creative ways to show appreciation and cultivate an attitude of gratitude in order to attract more positivity into our lives. There is one additional bonus card—Contentment—at the end of the deck.

Each card's message begins with a short, easy-to-remember affirmation. You can read them out loud, or simply repeat them in your head. Positive affirmations are simple yet powerful tools to help train our brains and our attitudes toward a more positive way of looking at life. They're especially helpful if you're prone to thinking negatively about yourself, and can't seem to stop destructive patterns. Saying or thinking an affirmation when a negative thought pops up helps us disrupt negative thought processes, and keeps us focused on the positive. They help cultivate self-awareness so we are better able to see our thoughts objectively. Over time, your mind will automatically function in a more constructive way, and you will begin to enjoy better self-esteem and more contentment.

Following each affirmation is a brief story that helps explain the imagery on the card, and how it pertains to our own lives. Ask yourself what you're attracted to in each picture, and spend a few moments seeking out the details. After you look at the cat, try to make up a story about it in your mind. Imagine what each kitty might have been doing before they were captured in paint, and what they will do afterwards. Carry this image with you throughout the day, looking back at the card if necessary. This will help you foster creativity, and see the world in a more whimsical way.

Each card offers simple suggestions or

insights on how you can apply the message to your own life. Read them through, pick one that stands out for you, and try to incorporate it into your day. Following this is a targeted exercise that will help you experience the message of the card in a more concrete way.

For an overall daily practice, choose a single card at random. For a random draw, shuffle the deck and hold it in your hands for a few moments while clearing your mind. Then choose a card, letting intuition guide you. Pick a card from the top or the bottom, or cut the deck and pick from the middle, whichever feels right for you. Read the affirmation, and either commit it to memory, or place the card somewhere you will see it several times a day. During the day repeat the affirmation, either through memory or by pulling out the card and reading it again. Repeat as many times as possible. At the end of the day, return the card to the deck and spend a moment to send a brief thought of gratitude to the universe.

For targeted use, sift through the deck until you find a card that speaks to you, or choose one that pertains directly to an issue you are dealing with. Read the insights and let them guide you to a better understanding of that issue. Use the exercise to help cement the card's message in your mind. Repeat the affirmation frequently throughout the day, and look at the image to focus your attention on the message. Carry the card with you or keep it on display as long as you need to, and when you're ready return it to the deck with an attitude of thankfulness and affection.

Just for fun, or for a pick-me-up any time, look through the cards one at a time just to enjoy the artwork. Pick a card that catches your attention to display in a spot where you'll see it frequently. Looking at it will remind you to smile and not take life so seriously.

Remember, life is beautiful, magical, and full of wonderment.

Always appreciate your beautiful, magical, wonderful life.

The Cards

🍃 INSPIRATION 🍃

Beauty

I am the beautiful that is right for me.

We all know that one person who radiates personality and charm. You want to be around them, and they light up a room when they walk in. They may not look like the fashionable ideal we see in the media, but their personality shines through, and makes people feel happy in their presence. They're comfortable with themselves, and appreciate their own individual sparkle. We're all beautiful, every single one of us, and it's our individuality that makes us so.

Stepping into the beauty of nature is like a balm to the soul. It exists in infinite diversity, in every color, shape, and size you could ever dream about. From the tiniest clover to the rarest rose, from the silky fur of a fox to the delicate tracery of a bat's wing, nature unveils itself in unending ways. Every living wild thing is perfectly content, and completely whole just as it is.

Diversity is the beauty ideal in nature, not conformity. Nature presents itself in ways that everyone can admire!

It's time to rethink and redefine beauty. True beauty is individual, and everyone is an individual. Celebrate what makes you different from everyone else. Your confidence will shine, drawing admirers like a moth to a flame!

Embracing Your Personal Beauty

- Be kind to yourself. No one is judging you as harshly as you are judging yourself.
- Stop striving for perfection. Perfection is the realm of the immortals, not humans. We're by definition not perfect—embrace that.
- Find your own signature style and dress to make yourself happy.
- When you find that negative voice in your head saying you don't measure up, reply with the affirmation: "I am the beautiful that is right for me."

Inspiration from Nature

Next time you're outside look for something small that you find aesthetically pleasing that you can pick up and bring home with you. A pinecone or unusually patterned rock, a feather, acorn, seed pod, or anything else that catches your eye. Put it in an out of the way nook, but somewhere you'll notice it often. As you glance at it throughout the day, remind yourself that true beauty is natural. True beauty is diverse. True beauty is free. Your beauty is individual, precious, and unique, a physical manifestation of the diversity of life. Celebrate that!

Flight

I am capable of anything I put my mind to.
I trust in my ability to succeed.

Starting out on a new endeavor can be exciting, with the anticipation of new adventures and experiences to enjoy. When trying something new, it's normal to worry a little about the path ahead, and wonder how things will turn out. For some people the unknown is a place full of possibilities, and they leap ahead trusting in their ability to cope and thrive. For others a fear of the unknown can hold them back on their path through life, or even stop them from starting out. We can't discover our full potential unless we're willing to take a little risk and trust the universe to be working for our best possible outcome.

Humans have always regarded birds in flight with awe. A seemingly delicate arrangement of feather and flesh, they soar with confidence. They're not afraid of falling, and they don't look down. They're fully, passionately, and fearlessly committed to the moment.

Don't let worry hold you back from experiencing a joyful and meaningful life. Instead of asking, "What if I fail?" ask yourself, "What if I succeed?" Sometimes you just need to take a leap of faith, and trust in your ability to deal with whatever life throws your way. If things don't turn out the way you expect, you can always choose another path. There is no such thing as failure, just an opportunity to seek another solution. On the other hand, if you don't try, you'll never know the possibilities you're capable of.

Coping With Fear

- Know that you're not a failure if you're fearful. Everyone is fearful sometimes! The secret of successful people is not that they don't fear, but that they can move past it. Accept fear as inevitable and not as a character flaw.

- Successfully dealing with fear is not a talent you must be born with, it's a skill you can learn. Everyone has the potential to deal with their fears. That means you too. You CAN overcome!

- Plan ahead, and lay the groundwork for success, taking things one step at a time.

- Give yourself permission to fail. If you fail, so what? The worst has happened, and you survived!

Soaring Above Our Fears

We all have the capacity to show great courage. Even a small bird can be seen attacking a hawk or a crow until the larger bird gets the message and flies away. Next time you find yourself feeling fearful, imagine yourself as a bird, small yet fierce, agile and determined.

Fortitude

I AM strength, I AM ability, I AM perseverance.

I can do anything I have to do no matter how hard.

♦ Fortitude ♦

Life can be difficult, but coping skills can be learned, and we must never feel that we need to tough it out alone. At times like these look to the tiniest denizens of the forest. A hummingbird is hardly bigger than a drop of rain, yet can weather the most devastating of storms. A beaver can divert a stream, changing its entire environment. These little ones don't quail against hardship or hard work; they simply know what they have to do and they do it.

This dainty unicorn cat stands strong against the approaching storm. It has seen them come and go before, and knows the good weather will always come again. The lightning, once so terrifying to one so small, now exhilarates and challenges. The forces of nature are awe-inspiring indeed, but this little unicorn cat knows it has the strength to persevere!

Dealing With What Life Throws at You

- Challenge yourself to take action. Remember that procrastination will not solve a problem, it only puts off the inevitable.
- Look at challenges as learning experiences, and use them as an opportunity to strengthen and grow.
- Never be afraid to ask for help! We do our best to help our loved ones out when they need it, so remember they're there for you too.

Inspiration from Nature

Imagine an approaching thundershower. As the storm nears the light dims, and the wind picks up speed. In the distance you hear a rumble of thunder, and a feeling of energy charges the air. The rain starts, at first just a few drops, and the temperature begins to fall as the rain comes down harder. You step inside, to watch the fury of the storm from the safety of your home. As the wind gets stronger and the lightning intensifies, you feel a sense of awe at the power of nature. Now imagine the storm abating, the wind dropping, and the sun slowly showing its face again. Suddenly the air is fresh and the grass is crisp and green. The birds are singing again and the squirrels are scampering. Even the most delicate looking of creatures had no problem surviving what nature threw at them. Next time you feel like a butterfly in a rainstorm, remember that you have the strength to not only survive, but thrive.

Growth

I will focus my energy on manifesting positivity in my life.

The smallest acorn can grow into the mightiest oak tree. While it might seem a magical process, it's really the inevitable result of nothing more than the right conditions. When nature is in harmony all things work together to support optimum growth, from the tiniest budding leaf to the majestic forest canopy. Nature in full bloom is an example of what can be accomplished when all living creatures manifest the best of their potential. All living things are an integral part of the growth and success of their environment.

A feeling of being stuck in life is something most of us can relate to. Sometimes a period of quiet inactivity is just what we need, but when we start to feel like we're going nowhere instead of resting, it's time to take stock of how we're managing our lives. Sitting around waiting for things to get better seldom results in positive change. It's always possible to change ourselves for the better, even if it takes many small steps to get to our goal. While the journey may be daunting, if you put one foot in front of the other and never give up, you will get to your destination. If you never try, you will never get there at all.

Cultivating Personal Growth

- Just like an oak tree can't grow overnight, a good outcome in life takes time, and is worth the effort. Life is meant to be a journey, not a destination.

- Consider that your life is a work in progress, and there is always room for improvement. As humans we have an infinite capacity to learn and change. Be humble and acknowledge the possibility that life still has lessons for you.

- Use difficult times to foster growth, appre-

ciate the lessons life throws at us and strive to do better.
- Mentoring and supporting others raises us all up collectively. Kindness costs nothing, but creates a ripple effect that enriches all our lives.

Growing Our Seeds of Potential

Imagine your heart is a small seed. We are all born with this seed, but we aren't told what kind of seed it is. As we grow, we experience all kinds of things both positive and negative that can affect it. As we grow, so does our heart. With each kindness we perform, every positive thought, and every time we are brave in the face of adversity, we strengthen and nurture our hearts. It's not what happens to us in our lives that determine how our hearts grows, it's how we react to these things. This is why some people can experience great hardship and loss and remain loving and optimistic. Strive always to water the seed of your heart with positivity, and your spiritual growth will be built on a solid foundation.

Metamorphosis

My limitless potential is just waiting for the right moment to be released.

Metamorphosis

From a lowly, earthbound creature to a gorgeous air bound jewel, the metamorphosis of a caterpillar into a butterfly is surely one of nature's most breathtaking and beautiful transformations. This is nature's ambition at its finest, a tiny and inspiring work of art.

As humans, we sometimes forget the huge potential we all have within us to change and grow.

Never Doubt Your Capacity for Change

- Look back over the years and see how many times your life has changed. Your life going forward has the same potential for change as before, so don't despair if you're going through a rough time and you feel stuck. Change is inevitable, and you will most definitely experience it again.

- Stop defining yourself by your current

situation. Most of us have big dreams yet we discount them as unobtainable. But no matter what you dream of, it's always possible to get there.

- Identify what needs to change in your life in order to reach your goal, and make a plan of action. Unlike the butterfly, our lives offer us a multitude of possibilities and paths to our goals!

- Never view a failure as a reason to give up. Setbacks help us learn, grow, and give us perspective on our lives.

- Be patient. Like a caterpillar inside a chrysalis, it takes time to bring about the fruits of our ambitions. Stick to your path, and never rush.

Action Plan

No matter how lofty our ambitions, we all must make the decision to simply start working toward them. Look to nature for inspiration and reassurance. Consider the lovely maple tree, which changes from green to blazing red overnight in response to a simple change in temperature. Don't discount the possibility that your goals may be realized quickly when the right conditions fall into place! If you're losing patience, remember our caterpillar. Sometimes it's necessary to withdraw and spend time in reflection before we can reemerge energized and ready to take on the world. You have the potential to be anything—never give up!

Mystery

I embrace the unknown as a source of opportunity.

🍃 Mystery 🍃

The forest at night is a mysterious place, coming alive with countless nocturnal creatures that go unseen during the day. As creatures of the day, we don't set foot into the night without a twinge of unease. Surrounded by eerie calls of unfamiliar animals and ominous rustlings in the undergrowth, we can't help but feel a little frightened.

While strange for us, the nighttime is comforting for those out and about under the moonlight. Sharpened senses easily see through the darkness that is opaque and obscuring to us. And oh what wonders we might see if we brave that darkness! Entire species that go unnoticed during the day grace the deep woods with their presence. Glowing insects weave trails of phosphorescence in the undergrowth. Flowers that only bloom under the moon release exotic scents into the cool air. If we always choose perceived safeness over adventure and new experiences, we only see half of what the world has to offer.

Stepping Into the Unknown

- If you are frightened to set out on a new venture, try to imagine the worst-case scenario. It's often not as bad as we envision.

- Take an honest look at your fear and ask yourself if it's truly grounded in reality. Try to differentiate between real issues, and an imagination run wild.

- Bolster your courage by stepping outside your comfort zone once in a while. Trying unfamiliar things may be scary but as you successfully deal with new initiatives in your life, you'll gain confidence.

Demystifying the Mysterious

When was the last time you took a walk at night? Life doesn't stop when the sun goes down, and taking a stroll in the dark is a good way to experience a whole other side of the world. Look up at the sky, and see how beautiful the moon and stars are. Breathe the cool night air and feel how refreshing it is. Listen carefully to the unfamiliar sounds around you. During the day we don't give a second thought to the noises around us, but at night the darkness can make even the most innocuous sound seem ominous. Just because something is unfamiliar does not make it dangerous or unnatural. Remember, all things that come out at night are in their element, just as you are during the daytime. As you continue on, feel yourself becoming more receptive to the mystery around you. The enveloping darkness will begin to be a comfort, and your senses will attune and adapt to help you experience the night more fully. As you return home and enter back into the light, remember the comfort the night holds now that it's more familiar.

Nurture

I love, support, and nurture those in my life.

I am committed to bringing out the best in everyone, including myself.

Animal parents are fiercely protective. They do their best to keep their children safe, comfortable, and nourished. A mother bird will sit on her eggs for weeks until the chicks are big enough to break their shells. They emerge tiny and weak, and count on her to look after them until they're big enough to fly from the nest. While childhood in the wild can be brief and dangerous, animal babies can always count on their parents to keep them safe. They can thrive and grow, without ever doubting for a moment that they are loved. And when they've grown up and are ready to become independent, they are fully prepared for all that life requires of them. Not only do they grow up in an atmosphere of love and affection, they're also taught the skills they need to have in order to survive.

Creating the conditions for success for our

children is a powerful way to change our world for the better. Just like a parent in the wild, we can all do our best to help our children grow up to reach their full potential. Children who are brought up with kindness, love and patience become kind, loving and confident adults. It's also important to nurture ourselves. Remember, we have limitless potential to grow and change for the better; we just need to create the conditions to help support one another.

Kindness Means Everything

- In order to support others, we should remember to be kind to ourselves. Feeling our best is an important tool for helping us deal with others. When you make your well-being a priority, you'll be better able to deal with others in a patient, loving way.

- Children should always be treated lovingly, and discipline should be used as a learning experience. Doing so will teach them that you are dependable and love them unconditionally. Nurturing a child with kindness helps them to step out into the world as a cheerful child, confident adolescent, and compassionate and strong adult.

- One of the best things you can do for your loved ones is to simply be there for them. Let them know you're always willing to lend an ear when they need to talk, and listen to them without judgment.
- A kind word or hug can make all the difference in someone's day. If you make even one person's life better today, who knows what greater positivity that will lead to.

Making the World Better is Easy, One Person at a Time

Right now, this very day, you can help make the world a better place. You are so powerful that you can make the day better for someone you don't even know! Smile at the clerk in the grocery store—they've seen enough grumpy customers today! The people you treat kindly will carry it with them for the rest of the day, and will feel inspired to pay it forward. You can get your family members involved too, and make a game of creating new ways to support each other. Try slipping a funny note into a family member's lunch, or leave an encouraging note pinned to the fridge. A reminder that you're thinking of someone is always welcome, and they'll be inspired to carry that warm and fuzzy energy to others throughout their day.

Patterns

I can look beyond the chaos around me and see meaning and purpose in my life.

Patterns

When we look around while outside in nature a quick glance presents a riot of seemingly disorganized life. The sheer diversity presented to our senses is beautiful, but at first impression can appear as chaotic. Underneath all the blooming flowers, rustling leaves, and busy animals going about their business, an infinite progression of patterns keeps things organized and flowing. Once we dig down we can appreciate the omnipresent webs that interconnect all species into a dance of harmonic beauty. We begin to see the purpose and organization that keeps all life in perfect balance and can appreciate how order rules our existence.

Pay Attention to the Universe

- Patterns of behavior can be both negative and constructive. If you are experiencing the same unwanted outcomes in your life, look for habits to improve on or eliminate. Often we don't make the connection between the way we behave and the direction our lives take, and end up sabotaging ourselves unknowingly.

- One of the worst habits we can get into is thinking negative thoughts about ourselves. With time and practice, we can learn to mindfully monitor our thoughts and train ourselves to become more positive and happier people.

- Sometimes, patterns pop up in our lives as messages from the universe to pay attention, and be receptive to receiving wisdom. You might see the same number combination repeating itself in different areas in your life. Watch for repeating patterns and keep an open mind.

- Successful people all make use of patterns of behavior to encourage continued success. Small consistent changes in our behavior can have a cumulative effect and move you along your path to happiness.

Pay Attention, and Look Close

If you start to look closely enough you'll notice that patterns abound in nature, from the uniform cells of a honeycomb, to the more complex shape of a spider's web. Have you ever taken a good look at the center of a daisy and seen how it arranges itself in a spiral? This phenomenon is called the Fibonacci sequence in mathematics and can be found everywhere in nature. The scales on a pinecone are arranged thus, as is the spiral shell of a snail, and the petals of many flowers. At first glance there isn't much the same about all these different things, yet they are all united by being formed according to this one mathematical pattern. Look carefully for these connections between living things, and you will begin to see more and more how all of life is incredibly intertwined.

Spring

As sure as winter always makes way for spring's joys I will never lose hope even when all seems bleak.

Spring is a time for rebirth, a glorious time of frantic activity. Spring represents a return to order, and a reminder that all is right with the world. It tells us that there is always a light at the end of the tunnel, and that life is cyclical and eternal. It gives us hope and keeps optimism alive during the long, bleak winter. And it reminds us that life needs its slow times to regenerate itself.

Spring gives us an uplifting feeling that starts out subtle, often with only a change in the wind direction and a small rise in temperature. You can feel it in the air with that part of your ancestral soul that still remembers sleeping under the stars in the days of humanity's infancy. As the tender sprouts emerge from the ground, we wait with bated breath for blossoms to unfurl. Spring calls us to action, urging us to get outside and lose ourselves in pure joy.

Keeping an Optimistic Mental State

- Without the harshness of winter, spring cannot even be dreamed of. It's not possible for anyone's life to be perfect all the time. So look at the down times as periods of rest in preparation for something wonderful coming.

- If you're going through a rough patch, don't worry about the future. Nothing stays the same forever, including times of difficulty.

- Know that everything that happens is working for your greater good. Adversity makes us stronger and more resilient, allowing us to bear difficult times with patience and grace. It also makes the good times that much sweeter.

- Allow yourself to have fallow times without feeling guilty. Just as the stillness of winter gets the world ready to welcome spring, self-care and rest prepare us to re-enter the world with renewed energy and sense of purpose.

Bring a Little Spring Inside

Start with a good spring cleaning and declutter your house. You'd be surprised how much lighter you'll feel without piles of stuff weighing down the atmosphere in your home. A good clean will freshen it up and make it feel airier and lighter. Once your house is clean, opt for a few bright colors in your decor. A nice pop of green or vibrant pink will give your eye something uplifting to focus on. This applies to your wardrobe too! Decorating with live plants can help give your home a fresher feeling as well. It doesn't matter how small your place is, there's always room for a splash of greenery or a simple vase of fresh flowers.

Stars

I am just as important as everybody else.

My existence is crucial to manifesting the universe in its present state.

When we look up at the stars at night, we're amazed at their beauty. We're also overwhelmed by how remote they are, and how vast our universe is. As humans we have only a tiny part in the grand dance of existence, so we have a hard time wrapping our minds around how infinite our present reality is. Instead of acknowledging our small place in the universe, we tend to think of ourselves as the center of existence, which may blind us to the potential that's out there.

Being small in our universe doesn't mean we're unimportant. Everything that exists influences life around it. Your existence has an effect on others in myriad ways, and therefore each of us serves an important purpose. Our very actions shape our reality every day because the world would not be the same without each of us.

We Are Stardust

- If you're feeling overwhelmed or insignificant, remember that the universe came into being from a finite point and expanded over time to the glory that exists today. Over time conditions became perfect for you to come into being. Your existence is every bit as miraculous as the stars that give light and beauty to our skies at night.

- Remind yourself that there is more to life than what we're experiencing; there is infinite possibility out there. While humans need to remember that we're not the center of life in the cosmos, this humility doesn't devalue our role; it simply leaves our minds open to more expansive ways of seeing the universe.

- Find your sparkle. Every single person has a unique ability, so develop yours. Acquiring proficiency in something reminds us of our unique capabilities, and gives us a sense of pride and accomplishment.

YOU Are Important

Our importance can be measured by the positive impact we have on ourselves, our loved ones, and the world at large. Some days it can feel like our individual lives are inconsequential, but even the smallest good deed can spark a chain of events that can rock the world to its foundation. Think of moments from your childhood when someone treated you with patience, love and encouragement. All of us remember someone who made an everlasting mark on our lives. Now, think back to times when your actions made a difference in someone's life. Strive to be a star in someone else's universe. Mentor a young person, donate food or time to a local charity, or simply pick up the phone and call someone who may be waiting to hear from you.

☽ CONTEMPLATION ☾

Balance

My needs are as important as the needs of others.

I will not sacrifice my well-being for the sake of anyone else.

A balanced life is a harmonious life. It's that sweet spot where everything in your life is given exactly the attention it needs, and all the pieces click together. A balanced way of living doesn't sacrifice one aspect of our life to shore up another. It promotes health and wellness, harmony in relationships, and the energy to carry out the necessary day-to-day tasks.

Nature left to its own, accomplishes a glorious dance of equilibrium. Every single living creature has its place that is equally important to the success of the whole. A complex system of checks and balances keeps everything working harmoniously. In our own lives it's important to realize when we're putting too much energy into one area and not enough into others. We all know people who work too hard, consume too much, or spend money they don't have. It's important not to confuse passion with unhealthy obsession. Passion helps us achieve our goals, while obsessions have negative consequences.

Find Your Equilibrium

- Overindulging is often an attempt to fill a void in other areas in our lives. Unfortunately this only results in short-term gratification, and long-term harm to ourselves or our loved ones. If you find yourself indulging in harmful habits, ask yourself what's lacking in your life to cause you to look for a temporary fix.

- Remember, YOU are as important as everyone else. Always take time for self-care! Don't place yourself second in your priorities. In the long run you'll only hurt yourself, and often others can't or won't see or appreciate the sacrifices you're making for them.

- Conversely, don't over-justify your excesses. Saying "I deserve it" when you want to make a purchase you can't afford is self-sabotage. Find a better way to practice self-care that won't negatively impact your future.

Beautiful Balance

Let's all commit to preserving the environment in its pristine glory. This can be as simple as using reusable shopping bags, ditching the plastic straws, or taking the bus instead of your car. Advocate for taking less from nature, which helps the earth heal itself without our intervention. We need to stop prioritizing consumption as the only way to drive our economy. Sometimes humans forget that we evolved to be part of nature, not to rule over it. Remember, when you spend time in nature, leave nothing behind but footprints, and take nothing away but memories.

Courage

I have the ability to overcome and succeed.

I will not let fear limit my possibilities.

In times of crisis, the tiniest creatures have the internal strength to stand up and protect themselves or their young. Smaller birds will dive bomb hawks to encourage them to move along. Tiny animals like rabbits and mice will attack predators that find their hidden young. All creatures contain the potential for courage, and they use it when they need to. When the time comes to do what they need to do, they do it!

Humans on the other hand can find themselves paralyzed by fear. Fear-based living keeps us from reaching our potential. While it's comfortable for some of us to find our niche and stay in it, it prevents us from finding out what we are really capable of. Life should be thought of as an adventure, but you can't experience an adventurous life if you're scared to take a chance once in a while.

We all have the potential to be brave, although some of us may have forgotten it. When a crisis comes we can either rise to meet the challenge, or we can relinquish control and be buffeted by the winds of change. While being courageous does not guarantee the best outcome of a situation, it can help you maintain control over your life instead of having others decide your fate for you.

Digging Deep

- The simple realization that we are all capable of being strong and courageous is hard for some people to believe. Everyone is capable of inner strength, and that means you too.

- Don't let past hurts control your future. If you're afraid of public speaking because a classmate made fun of you in school, in a way that person is still controlling your life. Don't give your power away to anyone else.

- Deal with your fears, one small step at a time. Often becoming less fearful is a matter of practice. If you're afraid of crowds, try going for a walk once a day in a public space where there are a few people. Once you're used to being around other people you can move onto more crowded spaces. Exposure to your fear desensitizes you to it over time.

- Imagine how your life would change if you overcame your fear. Fear of public speaking can hold us back in our careers. Fear of being rejected can prevent us from creating meaningful relationships. Don't

give your current fear power over your future life.
- Never feel like a failure because you're fearful. Fear is a survival instinct, not a character flaw. We're fearful because we're human, not because we're personally flawed.

Overcoming Your Fears

First, identify the root cause of your fear. Often phobias can be traced back to specific events that we may have forgotten. While humans still retain some instincts as a holdover from our wilder past, many fears are learned. A fear of the unknown can manifest itself as a fear of the dark. Take some time outdoors by yourself to give yourself some time for honest introspection. Animals certainly feel fear, but they don't let it hold them back as we humans do. Just as a sparrow can persevere over a hawk, we have the power and strength to move past our fears.

Death

I let go of my fear of death and joyously live in the moment.

Death is inevitable, inescapable, and frightening for some of us to contemplate, yet is something we all have to experience one day. It's incredible that something that is such an intrinsic part of life is so mysterious and inscrutable. The simple truth is that no matter how much we try to see beyond the veil, as humans that knowledge is simply not given to us.

All living things come into being, fulfill their purpose in life, and in the end return to the ground. The discarded husk of every being is broken down and returned back into the ecosystem, which in turn promotes growth and supports the birth of future generations. The circle of life is beautiful and full of purpose.

The creatures of the forest don't worry about dying some day; they live in the moment and carry out the tasks they need to survive. Even those who are allotted only a short time on this earth don't waste it in worry. Unfortunately, the same is not true for many of us humans. We allow fear and worry to eat away at our peace of mind, letting something that has not yet come to pass diminish our present. We can't fully enjoy anything when we are afraid of losing it. We don't fully live if we are worrying about dying.

Letting Go of Fear

- Start to see yourself as an integral part of the cosmic dance of life. We are all part of the totality of existence, and no matter how small we may feel in the universe we have a role to play in the grand scheme of things. You are just as much a part of that eternity as every other living thing.

- Worrying about death won't prevent it from happening. Your job is to make the most of your every single moment on this earth. If you worry, you can't experience the present fully. No one knows why they've been put here on earth, but enjoying and experiencing life to the utmost honors the Creator's mysterious purpose.

- Just as worrying about our own death

dampens our enjoyment of our lives, worrying about losing another can prevent us from enjoying our relationships to their fullest. Enjoy your loved ones here and now.

- Remember, without death life is simply not possible. Death of the old makes way for the birth of the new. Your place here on earth is only possible because those before you passed away, handing the torch to a new generation.

Familiarizing Yourself With the Inevitable

In the past, humans would honor their ancestors in yearly rituals, allowing them to remain a part of family life. But in most modern societies, we do our utmost to remove any trace of death from our lives. No wonder we find it strange and frightening! If you feel fearful, find a natural object that is beautiful, but no longer a part of the living world. A seashell perhaps, or a pinecone, or even a skull of a small animal if you can find one. Place it in corner of your home where you will glimpse it from time to time. Remind yourself when you see it that death is normal, inevitable, and a part of the grand scheme of life. Strive to live life to the fullest in the here and now.

Depth

I will cultivate compassion for others by acknowledging there are reasons for the way they behave.

Look at a still pond—what do you see? Do you see the surface, with reflections of clouds? Do you see the floating plants that bridge the depths with the sky? Or can you see what's going on below the surface? All three views are accurate, and you can see all of them at the same time if you try. An old saying goes, "still waters run deep." That's true for the motives behind human behavior. It's easy sometimes to label people according to their actions, but there is always a reason behind everything we do, even if it's buried so deep we are not aware of it on a conscious level. Look past the facade that people wear; it's often there to shield the pain they feel inside. When we acknowledge this pain in others it helps us cultivate compassion, an essential step to spiritual growth. Once you feel compassion for someone who has hurt you, you can help them grow by treating them with understanding and love. And if they hurt you beyond what's acceptable for you, you can walk away without anger or regret. Once you begin to see the reasons behind negative behavior, you will come to realize that there are no evil people, just broken and damaged souls in need of help.

One of the worst injustices we can do to another is judging by appearance. Physical attributes are like reflections on the surface of a pond. Both can often hide what lies within. Closer to a person's heart is their actions. A fertile pond bottom will give birth to plants that grow strong to break the surface, in the same way a generous and peaceful heart will manifest actions that nurture and build others up. In helping others we make the world better for them, ourselves, and everyone who they come in contact with.

Cultivating Empathy

- If you have a habit of jumping to conclusions about people based solely on how they appear, remind yourself that life is impermanent, and a person's body is only clothing a soul wears for a brief time while experiencing the physical world. Strive to learn who a person really is, not who you think they should be based on what they look like.

- Try to treat others with compassion. While difficult people can be hard to react to in a positive way, knowing their behavior stems from past hurts can help you understand the motives behind what they do. When you can look past a person's behavior to see what really motivates them, you can help them find solutions to salve the hurt.

- Don't forget to look inside yourself for your own motives if dealing with bad habits and patterns in your own life.

Cultivating Awareness

Train yourself to look beyond the superficial by really taking notice of your surroundings. There is so much more to existence than meets the eye, but you have to learn how to look. When you look at a tree, can you see the seasons it took to grow? Can you feel its roots below the surface, breaking up the earth? Do you feel the presence of all the birds, beasts and insects that call that particular tree home? A tree is not just a thing, it's a living, breathing ecosystem that is part of a greater whole. Sensing these overlapping layers of existence enriches our experiences and allows us to connect more deeply with the interconnected universe.

Environment

I honor and appreciate our planet.
I do my upmost to sustain and nurture the environment.

Without doubt, human habits are the biggest challenge facing our beautiful planet Earth. Our economy is based on an unsustainable model that takes and takes and never gives back. We value things more than our living world, and there is continual push for greater consumption. Our modern society is based on collecting stuff, and that emphasis on purchasing is threatening the very future of human existence and our planet.

Nature at her best is balanced, self-sustaining, and truly represents the infinite variety of possibilities life can offer. Every single part of nature exists as an equally important part of the whole. It's only when man steps in and tries to manage things that nature becomes unbalanced. We've forgotten our place in the world, and we're tearing it down around us in a vain attempt to find meaning and fulfillment in our lives. It's time to take positive action to protect the Earth.

Restoring Balance

- We're currently stuck in a model of society that is wasteful, destructive, and unsustainable. Make a commitment to break with this model to live a life that honors our planet. Acknowledge your part in perpetuating wastefulness, and strive to do better.

- Get off the fashion treadmill. Fashions are arbitrary, decided by corporations for the sole purpose of selling more products. Following fashion trends allows you to be herded like sheep. Find your own style, and refuse to be part of the herd.

- Stop measuring yourself by society's standards of what constitutes success. There will always be people who are more materially successful than you. Your self-worth should not depend on what you own. True self-worth should be based on the quality of your character.

Make a Difference

While sometimes we feel so small in the grand scheme of things, big changes start with individuals. There are lots of small but meaningful ways you can help heal our planet, and your example can inspire others to do the same. Making change is easy! Walk whenever you can. Use reusable grocery bags. Ditch the plastic straws. Learn to cook from scratch, from real foods that don't come in wasteful packaging. If you have a yard, plant a garden and learn to compost. Above all else, simply commit to doing better. The future of our planet depends on those who appreciate nature and rise above consumerism. The planet will heal itself with or without us; it's up to us to make sure we don't end up as a footnote in its evolution.

Mindfulness

I will cultivate a quiet mind to fully experience the present.

Some days it feels as if we move through life in a state of barely controlled chaos. It seems like all the contrivances of modern life that were promised to make things easier are just overcomplicating things. We're often overstimulated and exhausted. There's always so much to do and not enough day to do it. When we do get a moment to settle down too often we spend the time in front of a screen. This isn't true living.

Spend time in a forest and you'll experience an enveloping sense of calm. In Japan they call this *shinrin-yoku,* or forest bathing. Time spent in nature washes the static from our weary brains, and restores a sense of peace and order to the soul. Next time you're in the wild look around, and see how every living thing is concentrating on the one thing they do best at any moment in time. Grass grows, flowers bloom, animals go about their day-to-day business, one task at a time. They're focused and energized, and living life wholly as nature intended. It's possible to bring this state of mind to your everyday life, through a practice known as mindfulness. Quite simply put, it's the state of being fully present in the moment. This isn't as easy to do you as you may imagine, especially since most of us are conditioned to constantly multi-task. But there are some simple techniques you can practice in order to help calm your thoughts.

Baby Steps to Tranquility

- Spend time away from your screen. Constantly flipping between screens on a computer or device can train your brain to crave constant stimulation. In time this can affect the way you think, making it hard to focus on one task at a time. If you find you can't sit still for more than a few moments without reaching for your phone to check your email or social media, that's a sure sign you need to cut back.

- Read a book. Reading helps calm the random thoughts that come and go, stimulates imagination, and gives the brain a good rest from the cares of the day. Electronic devices make reading convenient, but reading on a device is less than ideal because there's always the temptation to flip between your book and apps. If you would prefer not to read the traditional way, you can get a device devoted only to reading.

- Take the time to really enjoy your food when you're eating. Food is meant to be enjoyed, and deserves to have your full attention. Savor every bit that goes in your mouth, and be grateful for it.

- Several times a day, take a step into nature. This can be as simple as walking out the door for a few moments and taking a few deep breaths of air. Close your eyes, and feel how good it is to breath. If this isn't possible, head to a window. Look up at the sky, and for a few minutes let your mind just enjoy the view.

Nature Therapy

Find a quiet place in a natural setting. A backyard or city park is fine. Sit down on the ground if you can, and if you can lean against a tree, that's even better. Take a few deep breaths, and try to quiet your mind as best you can. If you feel unwanted thoughts popping up, acknowledge them and turn your attention back to your breath. Try to feel your surroundings with your individual senses as much as you can. Feel the fresh air as it fills your lungs, and let tension escape from your body with each breath. Feel the warmth of the sun on your skin. Hear the joyful music of rustling leaves, flowing water, or birdsong that surrounds you. When you're ready, open your eyes, and see how peaceful life can be when everything works in harmony and honors its purpose in life. Before you go back home, make sure to send a thought of gratitude out to your surroundings for this blessed moment of peace.

Silence

I remove the distractions of modern life to help me listen better to my authentic self.

Leaving the modern world behind and stepping into the forest feels like diving down into a cool, still pond. We don't realize how overbearing the constant noise that surrounds us is until we remove ourselves from it. While far from silent, the sounds that occur in nature are gentler and more soothing. The deeper into the forest you go, the quieter it becomes as the trees begin to insulate us from the outside world. What remains are sounds that are beautiful and a balm to our overstimulated lives. We can hear our own breath again, and our thoughts are protected from the noise and distractions we experience every day.

The constant chatter and noise of modern living fragments our concentration and keeps us focused on the external, instead of being mindful of our own thoughts and feelings. We grow addicted to background noise and feel uncomfortable without the constant distraction. When we never tune out the noise, it distorts our thinking and keeps our minds in a constant state of stimulation. The result is that our ability to focus on the here and now gets diminished, and we're left with a vague sense of unease when things are quiet. This state of mind removes our appreciation of the simpler things in life, and keeps us from finding a spiritual state of equilibrium.

Letting Your Spirit Speak

- If you're in the habit of always having noise in the background, shut it off for at least a few hours a day. Exposing ourselves to silence once in a while allows our brains to focus on the task at hand.

- Keep the electronics off during meals. Sitting down to eat in a nice quiet atmosphere helps us appreciate our food more, and stimulates social interaction. Make mealtime conversation time for you and your family. It will bring you all closer together and strengthen your relationships.

- If you're feeling stressed or overwhelmed, seek out quiet spaces. Try heading to a museum, park or library. At work, take a moment to step outside on your break and get some needed peace and quiet.

- Once you begin to get comfortable with a peaceful atmosphere, try meditating to further quiet your mind. Some people find the idea of meditating intimidating and difficult, but it's as easy as sitting still with your eyes closed for a few minutes. Make yourself as comfortable as possible, so you're not distracted by the position of your body. Close your mind, and breathe. Try to keep your mind as empty as possible, but don't get upset by random thoughts that pop in. Simply acknowledge them, and return your attention to your breath. This helps remove the chatter from within, to return our minds to a calm and focused state.

Experiencing Healing Silence

Occasionally, it's important to seek out wild spaces and reconnect with nature's music. The sound of running water, the breeze in the trees, and the melody of birdsong soothes and invigorates. If it's impossible for you to get away from the city, head to a park, or try sitting outside at night when the sounds of human activity die down. Breathe deep, and let the lack of distractions help you reconnect with your thoughts. Let the silence wrap you in a cocoon of peace and quiet contentment.

Solitude

I will distance myself from the world in order to know myself more intimately.

Are you afraid to be alone? Sometimes it's scary being by ourselves, because it removes the distractions and validation provided by the people we surround ourselves with, and forces us to recognize our genuine selves. If you're used to relying on others for direction, setting out on your own path can be daunting. It's important to find time alone so you can really begin to learn who you are and what you want, away from the influence of others.

Some of us are so scared of being rejected, we try too hard to please others. We don't act like our genuine selves, and fall into the habit of ignoring our own needs and wants. In time, this can lead us to forget who we really are, and we begin to define ourselves by how we interact with others, and constantly seek approval from outside. Your worth isn't defined by what others think of you. Every living thing is important in itself because it has a purpose to play in the whole of creation. That means you too, although some days it doesn't feel like it. Without YOU the world would be entirely different. No matter how big or small our role in this life, it's important, and it matters. YOU matter. Spending time by yourself helps you understand who you really are. And if you find yourself overworked and overwhelmed by day-to-day life, you need time alone to recharge. You deserve this as much as everyone else!

Making Time for YOU

- Remember you are as important and deserving of time to yourself as all others in your life. Never feel guilty for insisting on "me time." You deserve it!

- If you find others in your life are demanding of your time, find non-confrontational ways to be alone. Picking up a book or putting in earphones is often a subtle enough signal to others that you're not interested in interaction at the moment. If this doesn't work, learn to walk away.

- We can't help others if we don't also take care of ourselves. Our loved ones deserve our support, energy, and attention, so taking time to recharge and rest benefits yourself and everyone else in your life

- Spending time alone forces us to see ourselves as we really are, not through the lens of other people's opinions. Self-esteem comes from within; it can't be given by others. Spending time alone takes a little courage, but in time you'll grow to be more at ease with your own company. Start with small steps, like going shopping on your own, or finding a cozy corner by yourself to read.

Step Out of the World for a Moment

Spending time in nature is a powerful tool for healing a wounded spirit. Being alone outside not only removes us from the influence of others, it also removes us from our daily lives in order to see ourselves with greater clarity. A solo hike in the woods or a walk through a park allows us to pass time without worrying about pleasing others. Removing ourselves from our habitual surroundings can help us see our obligations and relationships with a clearer perspective.

Sprout

I see the potential in everything, especially in me.

Sometimes it's hard to see the potential in things, especially when the going gets rough. It's hard to believe that a shriveled bulb holds the soul of a flower, waiting for the right conditions to grow and bloom. Even the most barren landscape holds the potential for beauty and transformation. You can see miracles waiting to happen everywhere if you look with your heart as well as your eyes.

Every single human soul holds the potential for growth and a higher purpose. It's important to remember that we never lose the capacity to improve our lives and the lives of those around us. Training our minds to look for the potential in every situation is a solid first step in manifesting abundance in our lives.

Finding Your Potential

- Acknowledge your strengths. Sometimes it doesn't feel like it, but we ALL have things that we are good at. That means you too!

- Don't measure your strengths by what society and other people view as valuable. Societal standards change with the wind. Instead of trying to keep up with arbitrary measures of success, seek your own path.

- Discover and develop your talent. Talent is simply the result of being interested in something enough to practice it consistently. There is never a limit to how much you can improve through practice.

- Acknowledge your weaknesses. Sometimes this takes a bit of soul-searching, but when you know what you need to work on, you can make a commitment to doing it. Ask yourself honestly, "how are my habits hurting me and my loved ones?" Strive to do better.

- Appreciate failure as a learning opportunity. Everyone fails at some point in their lives, and successful people use failure as an impetus to try harder. Don't let fear of failure keep you from trying new things.

Just for Fun

Watching a bulb sprout is a satisfying way of reminding ourselves of the hidden potential in our lives. If you have a yard, try planting bulbs in the fall that will sprout in the spring, like daffodils or hyacinth. When the winter snow melts, your yard will be a fragrant reminder of life's ability to endure. If you don't have the room or climate for that, try forcing a bulb inside. Before planting, hold your bulb in your hand and try to image the soul of the flower inside, waiting to burst into bloom. As it begins to flower, think of all the potential you hold inside yourself as a human being.

Winter

I know good things are awaiting me.

My patience will always be rewarded.

For many people winter is not their favorite season. If you live where it gets very cold the season of winter can seem long and lifeless. A quick glance at a snowy landscape reveals only the occasional glimpse of life—a squirrel visiting a cache, or a chickadee flitting among the bare branches. The creatures of the forest know how to prepare for lean times, and how to endure them. No matter how harsh the environment, nature always finds a way to celebrate and preserve life. Even the tiniest creatures cope and adapt, because it's in their nature to survive.

When faced with difficult times, remember that everything eventually passes. Sometimes all you can do is sit tight and wait, and know that you have the strength to get through it. Living through hardship will make you stronger, more resourceful, and better prepared the next time difficulties come your way. Knowing that we all suffer and that suffering is inevitable can be very freeing. It allows you to see that your troubles are not a punishment, but a human condition we all share. This knowledge can give us a feeling of compassion and kinship with others.

Alleviating the Suffering

- If you're having a bad day, and are having a hard time getting motivated to do anything, give yourself permission to just be. Don't feel guilty if all you've accomplished today is getting out of bed. Rest today, and let tomorrow deal with itself.

- Don't let the thing you are experiencing

define you. You may have failed at something, but you are not a failure. You're human, and humans by definition are fallible, so don't expect perfection from yourself.

- Now more than ever is the time for self-care. Enjoy that cup of tea, a bubble bath, or a chapter of your favorite book. Never feel guilty for being kind to yourself!

- This is a good time to practice compassion, because no one wants to feel judged when they're at their worst. This goes for you, too. Your experience is just as valid as everyone else's. Don't allow others to trivialize the pain you feel.

- When times are good, prepare for difficult times ahead. Develop coping skills that can get you through the rough patches, instead of habits that are destructive. Never be afraid to ask for help when you know you need it.

Visualization for Difficult Times

Imagine your life is a frozen, frigid landscape. You're floating above the ground, and the wind moves against you like an icy current, threatening to blow you away. You struggle and it's getting harder to find the strength to keep going. Now slowly imagine you're sinking down, below the surface of the snow. Immediately, the wind is gone. You're still cold, but a calmness has come over you. As you sink lower through the snow, you find yourself in a pocket of last summer's foliage. It's very still, and very quiet, and as you settle down you begin to feel the warmth from your core rising to the surface. Wrap yourself in this warmth. This is your inner strength enveloping you. Your ability to cope, survive, and thrive is inside you and always has been.

♥ COMFORT ♥

Adaptability

I accept change in my life, trusting that the things that are truly important will never fade away.

♥ Adaptability ♥

From the seasonal cycles that change the landscape in predictable patterns, to the awesome and chaotic power of weather to sculpt our world, nature is a restless force that constantly reinvents itself. Without change life would stagnate and new growth would not be possible. Life evolves over time, and sometimes the old has to be swept away to make way for the new. While things seem to constantly change on the surface, universal truths underpin our existence, creating an enduring foundation that our entire world is built on.

At times we find change scary, and we prefer to live our lives predictably and safely. We see change as destructive and do our best to prevent it from happening. Change reminds us that we are not always in control and that revelation can be frightening.

We need to remember that things change not to be destructive, but to support the continuity of life on our planet. In our own lives, an attitude of adaptability helps us adjust to new situations, and helps ensure a successful future.

Learning to See the Bigger Picture

- Fear of the unknown is something many of us struggle with. Since change will happen to us no matter what, it's better to embrace it as an opportunity than let it diminish our lives with fear.

- Change means a new opportunity is arising. Embrace that opportunity as a chance to learn and grow. The human experience teaches us that we are greatly successful at adapting to change and using it to help us thrive.

- Adaptability maintains life. It ensures the long-term survival of species, while at the same time manifesting diversity, which in turn supports life and stability. Our species has risen to prominence through its ability to adapt, and has in turn made its mark on the world in a way no other creature on this planet can.

Reminding Ourselves of the Permanence of Creation

A fossil on display in your home is a great way to remind yourself of how change works to create stability and growth in our lives. Each fossilized creature was once a living entity that left its mark on the earth to remind us that its contribution to life was enduring and important. Each tiny building block of life, no matter how small, was a crucial step in manifesting the world you see around you today. Your power to affect positive change in the world is limitless, so strive to create an enduring legacy you can be proud of.

♥ Affection ♥

Affection

I allow my love to flow freely to others.

I receive the love of others with gratitude.

Without question, our furry friends love each other and us! Anyone who has ever shared their home with an animal companion can tell you that they give love unconditionally. Animals love to cuddle, as some of us who always end up with a lap full of cat can attest to! Inspiring examples of unconditional love can also be found among our feathered friends, many of whom mate for life, rivaling the greatest of human romances. For animals, love is given easily, and affection is effortlessly appreciated.

Humans have every bit as much need for affection as our wild kin, but sometimes we need a nudge to overcome our inhibitions. We may have been brought up in families that are reserved, or that discouraged outward shows of affection. No matter, with a little practice we can all learn to open our hearts and show our loved ones how much we cherish and care for them, and let our affection flow freely!

Giving and Accepting Affection

- Some people are a little uncomfortable with expressing love physically, and that's OK. But do remember that we can all benefit from touch, and the more you share the gift of affection, the more comfortable you'll feel about it.

- We all show affection differently, so it's

important to be receptive to another person's love language. Keeping the lines of communication open can help you understand different styles of loving. Keeping your mind and heart open will help you recognize and appreciate being loved.

- If you have children, don't let a single day go by without hugging them. Being physically affectionate even with older children helps them grow up feeling loved and appreciated, and sets a good example for their future relationships.
- Communication is the best way to keep love flowing freely. If you're upset with a friend or partner, talk it out. And if someone is upset with you, encourage them to talk about it and really listen to what they are saying.

Loving Nature

In the past, humans lived in harmony with nature, viewing other living beings as equals and treating them with respect and compassion. Sometimes modern life removes us so far from nature that we forget our wild roots and our loving relationship with all living beings. Nurture a grateful relationship with nature and you will start to feel like a piece of creation again, as part of the miraculous web of diversity that exists on our planet. You will feel a kinship again with all beings, and your heart will begin to overflow with love. Carry that loving energy forward to the people you share your life with, and watch them bloom under your attention!

Autumn

I have a strong work ethic. I know what needs to be done, and I can do it!

♥ Autumn ♥

Autumn is the busiest time of the year in the wild. Nature's bounty is ready to be harvested, and her children take advantage of the cooler days to put away provisions for the long winter ahead. All wild animals that need to stock-pile food are at their busiest, and days are full of bustle and a great sense of purpose. By the turning of the leaves and the cool snap in the air, they know it's time for work, and they get to it! The brilliant hues of autumn are both a call to work, and a promise that nature will reward industry with ease and security during the winter. As the leaves fall and preparations wind down, all creatures begin to relax, drifting into winter with the comfort of a job well done.

Hard tasks can be daunting, causing us to doubt our energy or abilities to manage them. Stressing over tasks that need to be done takes our attention off the here and now, and prevents us from enjoying our lives in the present. You can't be happy if you're dreading a task you need to do! Even worse, shirking work can set us up for failure in the long run. While we all procrastinate from time to time, knowing how to get started is a skill that we can work on.

Developing a Strong Work Ethic

- When faced with a difficult task, fear of failure can paralyze us and keep us from even starting. You can complete what you need to do, no matter how hard it may seem. You are strong, capable, and able to accomplish anything you put your mind to.

- Except for a very privileged few, all of us need to work to maintain ourselves. Hard work is the rule, and not the exception, so stop feeling resentful and get on with your task.

- Start small, and be consistent. If all you can manage is one small thing at a time, it's a step in the right direction. Sometimes just getting started is the hardest part, and polishing off a small task will help you feel accomplished and motivated.
- Reward yourself for a job well done. When you accomplish something great, take time to celebrate! A reward is a great incentive to get working, so make sure to allow yourself to enjoy your accomplishments.
- Set goals and get organized. Break down tasks into logical steps, and write them down so you can check them off as you finish them.

Examples from Nature

Contemplate the many examples from nature that exemplify the ability to overcome daunting tasks one step at a time. A beaver can build a dam strong enough to divert an entire river, one stick at a time. Birds weave their nests from bits of grass and twigs, and rabbits dig impressive networks of tunnels with their tiny paws.

They don't pause to doubt their abilities, and neither should you! Never forget to remind yourself that you are capable, resourceful, and energetic enough to get the job done. You can do it, you will succeed!

Faith

I trust in a Higher Power working for the greater good of myself and all living beings.

♥ Faith ♥

Where humans falter, nature never loses faith. Life can be harsh and unpredictable, yet all wild creatures under heaven live their lives as they were designed, without questioning their future. Every living being has a purpose to serve and we honor the Creator by living our lives to the best of our abilities, trusting in divine purpose. We all have a part to play in the miraculous dance of life, and while we might not see what part we play as individuals, we need to have faith that the universe is continually working toward the good of all.

Humans are curious creatures and have a drive to understand the inscrutable, wanting to control the unpredictable. Yet just a quick look outside shows us how harmonious life can be when every living creature, animal and plant, lives in the moment and leaves the future in the capable hands of Mother Nature. The complexities of life on Earth, the beautiful interconnections and patterns that underscore all of existence, are proof of the wisdom of the universe. We need to remember that we're only a small piece in the puzzle, but without us the puzzle would be incomplete. Without your existence the cosmos just wouldn't be the same. You're that important!

Learning to Trust in a Higher Power

- Allow yourself the realization that as humans, we may never be allowed a glimpse behind the veil. Try as we might, it may not be within our abilities to get a definite answer to all the mysteries of life. It's impossible that our astonishingly complex and beautiful universe was born randomly, so we must know that there is more to life than what meets the eye and trust that our Creator is always present. Our job is to enjoy the wonderful here and now that we've been given, and allow our destinies to unfold as they are designed to do.

- None of us can see what the future has in store for us, but we all have the the ability to use our lives to learn and grow. So ask yourself, is this thing that I'm doing helping make myself and the world a better place? Every action we take should be a mindful step toward the betterment of ourselves, our loved ones, our communities, and ultimately our planet. When we act as though we're part of a community we can't help but build a better and brighter future for all. When we work toward a better tomorrow for all living creatures, we're aligning ourselves with the goal of the Creator in manifesting a beautiful, complex, and awesome reality.

- No one individual is born with any guarantee of a perfect, conflict-free life. Setbacks along the way are not proof against the existence of a Higher Power, but are given to us as opportunities to strengthen our minds, bodies, and spirits. The fact is, we are all born with everything we need to navigate this journey through life. The cosmos is so concerned for our well-being that it has given us all the conditions we need to be happy, and stepped back to give us room to explore our lives on our own terms, and in our own time. How wonderful is that! Like a loving parent gives a child the tools they need to thrive and be independent, our loving Creator has given us everything we need to live our best lives and take care of ourselves on our own.

Regaining Your Faith

Faith is that special feeling that tells us no matter what, things will be ok. It gives us hope for the future, and connects us with loved ones who have passed on. It gets us through the tough times, and comforts us when we're feeling lonely or sad. If you're finding it hard to find faith, just look around at our beautiful planet. Think about all the conditions that had to arise just to bring forth life on our Earth—it's impossible that that happened just by accident! All life is interconnected in a way that shows us there is more to our existence than meets the eye. We're all a crucial part of the balance of life, placed here with care and attention for a great purpose. We need only to enjoy the lives we've been given, and appreciate our perfect place in the universe, grateful to help fulfill the Creator's great plan.

Family

♥ Family ♥

*My family loves, cherishes, and accepts me as I am.
I love, cherish and accept my family unconditionally.*

Families in nature come in all kinds of forms. Some extend to packs that include multiple generations, with all members helping to raise the youngest. For others it seems like one parent takes on all the responsibility, like the gentle deer who raises her fawns without benefit of a fatherly influence, or the male seahorse who gestates and births his children. Some animals mate for life, raising their offspring as a shared effort. There is no one definition of family in nature. Instead there is an arrangement that works to ensure the best possible benefit for all individual species.

The same is true with human relationships. It's wonderful that times are changing and more unconventional family arrangements are beginning to find acceptance.

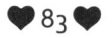

Your family members are those who appreciate you with all your quirks and flaws. They encourage you to realize your full potential, and are always there for you when you need it. They don't judge you for being different, and in fact will help you celebrate the things that make you unique. Family is pure love and acceptance.

Celebrating Your Unique Family

- No two families are alike. There is no "normal" arrangement to aspire to, so be assured your family is perfect for you.
- Don't let a day go by without reaching out to at least one family member to let them know how much you appreciate them.
- Don't feel that your family is an exclusive club. Especially around holidays, be willing to invite others to share in your companionship. Love is infinite and there is always room for one more.
- If you're a parent, be mindful that your children look to you to learn tolerance and acceptance. Helping them to see the beauty in all kinds of different relationships is a wonderful gift you can give them.

Creating a Family Nature Memorial

One fun way to create a tribute to a family milestone is to plant a tree. Joyful occasions like a new baby or a wedding, or more serious ones like a move or even a death, can be memorialized in this way. As a tree grows it marks the passage of time and provides joy for the senses. Its spreading branches are joined by one trunk, reminding us that we're all individuals, but all tied together by bonds that are strong and loving. If you don't have access to your own land for a project like this, consider donating to a local conservation organization in your family's name.

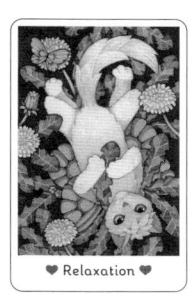

♥ Relaxation ♥

Relaxation

I make my well-being a priority and blissfully enjoy a moment without care.

It's no secret that our furry friends know how to relax. If you've ever lived with a cat or dog you know they like to sleep most of the day. It's much the same in the wild, although when we see an animal in its native habitat, it's nearly always hustling and bustling about. That's because animals at rest are hidden to us, protected by camouflage and a talent to remain still. What we don't see are the birds quietly resting on branches, heads hunched down and buried in ruffled feathers or the squirrels relaxing in the fork of a tree. This gives the illusion that life in the wild is constantly busy, never slowing down for a moment. We can only see one side of the coin.

So many people don't make rest a priority and work too hard and too long. We end up burned out and with failing health. The simple truth is we need to rest in order to be happy and healthy. We need to find balance in our lives, and allow ourselves downtime without feeling guilty.

Take Time to Recharge

- You deserve to put your feet up once in a while, and you need to. We're not at our best if we don't give ourselves time to refresh our bodies, minds, and spirits. Working ourselves to the point of exhaustion may seem admirable to some, but in the long term this effort is not sustainable.

- Don't feel the need to make everything perfect. It's OK to let the dishes pile up at the end of a busy day. Or, enlist the help of a family member. Never feel reluctant to ask for help if you need it. Families exist to support each other, so make sure the load is distributed evenly.

- If you have a big task at hand, make sure you give yourself enough time to finish. Don't make unrealistic promises to those you're working for, and most of all be honest to yourself about the scope of your abilities.

- When you need a rest, give yourself permission to enjoy your time alone. Turn off your phone and don't worry how others are getting along without you. Set aside your work and obligations for a moment. Go outside for a walk. A little leisure will help our work in the long run, as we're able to approach it with a clear head and rested body.

Learning to Make Yourself a Priority

If you're one of those people who works themselves to the point of burnout, it's important to make your rest a priority. We can't perform to the best of our abilities if we're mentally and physically exhausted, so consider downtime an investment in your future performance. Scheduling leisure time is a great way to fit relaxation time into your agenda. If your kids are running you ragged, designate one night a week as "me time." Enlist someone to babysit, and take some time just for yourself. If you're burning out at work, honestly look at whether your overwork is your own choosing. Don't work through breaks, and leave at quitting time. If your workplace culture pressures you to stay late and skip breaks, refuse to get caught up in office politics. No job is worth damaging your health for, so set firm boundaries and stick with them.

♥ Scent ♥

Scent

I surround myself with the scents of nature to evoke memory, promote healing, and enjoy peace of mind.

Spring is a riot of unfolding colors and delicious scents. Tantalizing aromas of early bloomers like lily of the valley and hyacinth wake our senses up from the long winter, calling us to come outside and enjoy the changing weather. As summer rolls around, these spring blossoms make way for showy perfumed flowers like lilacs and roses. Autumn's scents are more subtle and crisp, stirred up by feet crunching through leaves and blustery winds shaking through fresh pine boughs. Winter brings wood smoke from fireplaces wafting on the breeze.

Scent is the sense that powerfully evokes past memories. Our brains make strong connections between smell and the things we experience in our lives. A single whiff can transport us back in time to relive a memory that may have been long forgotten. The scent of a particular perfume in a crowd can instantly bring to mind a particular person, no matter how long it's been since you've seen them. The scent of gingerbread baking can transport us back to a childhood memory of Christmas. Natural essential oils are a gentle way to experience aromatherapy.

Natural Scents

- Natural essential oils are a gentle way to enjoy natural scents and their health benefits. If you like floral scents try jasmine, rose, or lavender. If you like the smell of citrus try bergamot. For those with more exotic tastes, try patchouli or sandalwood. For a homey cozy feel, opt for cinnamon or cloves.

- Essential oils can be diffused in your home to help cleanse the air, promote relaxation, and positively affect your moods. If you're feeling tired or nauseous, peppermint can provide a quick pick-me-up or calm an upset tummy. Eucalyptus oil can clear a stuffy nose, while tea tree can help freshen the air in a musty room. Lavender is a time-tested aid for insomnia, while any kind of citrus can energize you.

Blossom Bath Ritual

Nothing is more relaxing than a hot perfumed bath, and homemade scented Epsom salts will take relaxation to another level. Epsom salts are widely available and help calm tension and ease tight muscles. For a relaxing soak, add about five drops of lavender essential oil and a small handful of dried lavender flowers to one cup of Epsom salts. Rub the flowers between your palms as you add them to crush them up a little, and shake all ingredients together before storing in an airtight container. Run yourself a nice hot bath, and add about a quarter cup of your salts mixture. If possible, dim the lights and light a candle. As you soak in the hot, scented water take joy in how lovely it feels, and let the aroma waft away the troubles of the day.

Sleep

I release the cares of the day and effortlessly drift away into sleep.

♥ Sleep ♥

Effortless, rejuvenating sleep. It's something we all need, but so many of us find elusive. Not so our furry friends! Whether a kitten curled up in a convenient nook, or stately lion sprawled out in the shade, all creatures big and small have no difficulty drifting away and enjoying peaceful, restful sleep.

Our ancestors enjoyed the same ability to sleep as the animals around them. They were attuned to the rhythm of the sun and moon, finding themselves in harmony with the rest of nature, and slept and rose with the setting and rising sun. Today our modern life seems to do anything but promote good sleep. We find ourselves too busy to get all we need to get done in one day, and so go to bed far too late. We work by unnatural schedules, forcing us to rely on alarm clocks to wake us up before we're fully rested. We forget that quality sleep is crucial to our health and mental well-being.

Promoting Quality Sleep

- Practice good sleep hygiene. There are several bad habits we can get into that prevent us from falling asleep quickly or getting quality sleep. Watching TV or browsing on a device or a computer can prevent you from falling asleep. Turn your TV off early, and put your device away. Electronics have no place in your bedroom.

- Make your bedroom an inviting space, and reserve it for sleep only. Paint your walls a soft dreamy color to avoid stimulating your mind before bed. Sleep in a room that's as dark as possible, since any light that makes its way in can disrupt sleep. If your room is too bright opt for an inexpensive sleep mask. Aromatherapy can also help you drift off.

- Reserve a half hour or so before bed for reading. Reading helps our minds focus on one thing, calming the multi-tasking mode so many of us adopt during the day. It also helps us escape reality for a bit, which is especially helpful if you're suffering from anxiety. A good book takes our focus off our problems, lightens our mood, and calms the body.

- After bad bedtime habits, worry is the most likely thing to keep you lying awake at night. There are many ways to deal with anxiety naturally, like the exercise that follows. Remember, worrying about tomorrow won't help you deal with the problem any better, it will only ruin your sleep and take away the serenity of the present.

Breathing Green

If you're having trouble falling asleep, this simple breathing exercise can help you clear your mind and relax your body. Lie on your back, with your hands wherever they are the most comfortable. Close your eyes, and consciously release the tension from your body, starting at your feet and working your way up to the crown of your head. Once your body is comfortable, slow your breathing down, paying attention to each breath. Feel how the air coming in fills your chest, and carries on down into the belly. Now, imagine as you breath in, the air is a lovely shade of green, filling you with a calming natural energy. As you breath out, imagine this spent breath escaping your body as a grey cloud, containing all your worries and stress. Alternate breathing in green, and breathing out grey. With each breath in the green energy spreads in your body, healing and calming. With each breath out you become more relaxed and peaceful. Focusing on our breath helps calm anxiety, and helps us feel cleared of negativity. Let go of your worries, and feel yourself drift away into blissful sleep.

Sun

My heart is energized with every rising of the Sun.
My heart is light, bright, and shines with positive attitude.

♥ Sun ♥

The Sun is the ultimate source of life for our planet. Without its shining energy life on Earth simply wouldn't be possible. It's no wonder so many cultures worship the Sun as a deity. In the far reaches of our history our ancestors welcomed the day with awe and reverence. They carefully tracked the majestic movement of the Sun's dance with the seasons, creating rituals to celebrate milestones in the wheel of the year. The ancient Egyptians worshipped the Sun god Ra, who is sometimes depicted as rising out of a lotus blossom growing from the primordial Earth. Over time the Sun has lost its mystery for us, and we now know the science behind its radiance. While the Sun is no longer the mystery it once was, it's every bit as awe-inspiring today, as it supports our sustenance, health and well-being.

Light Up Your Life

- Try to get a little Sun exposure every day. Sunlight has been shown to boost chemicals in our brains that promote happiness, and also helps our bodies make vitamin D, which is crucial for our health. While it's important to be mindful of too much sun exposure, a few minutes a day can boost our moods and contribute to our health.

- Once in a while try to get up early enough to enjoy watching the sunrise. Early morning sunshine is fresh and light, bathing the world with a rosy glow that encourages us to get up and get on with our day. It sparks creativity and imparts a sense of optimism.

- The noontime Sun is warm and energetic, and marks the Sun's highest position in the sky. It's also the hottest part of the day, giving us a needed boost of energy during the winter. In very hot climates it's a good time to take a rest and recharge before you go on with your day.

- Sunset's gorgeous warm hues encourage us to settle down for the night, and boosts feelings of gentle happiness and well-being. Take advantage of this calming energy to relax with friends or family, enjoy a nice cup of tea, or read a good book.

Attuning to the Sun

A personal morning positivity ritual offers a great way to boost your energy, and will leave you refreshed and ready to face your busy day. Sunrise is the best time for this, but you can do this at any time in the morning. Find a spot where the sunlight can shine directly on your face, either outside or through a window. With your eyes closed, appreciate how good the sun feels on your face, and feel the warmth being absorbed into your very core. Feel this warmth comforting and soothing your spirit, and notice your mood lift as you experience this cozy feeling. As your mood elevates, feel how grateful you are to be experiencing this moment, and send a thought of gratitude out to the Universe. Open your eyes, take a deep breath, and go on with your day.

Tenacity

I am strong, resourceful, and adaptable.

I am able to navigate the storms of life, attaining my goals through tenacity.

♥ Tenacity ♥

No matter where you look, creatures make their homes in the harshest of climates. Even places where the challenges of life seem insurmountable, life not only exists, but thrives. From the hottest desert to the deepest trench in the ocean, life always finds a way to express itself. You can see this in the way the soft roots of trees work their way around the rocks of the earth. Given the smallest of opportunity, life will find a way.

We're all familiar with the expression "all good things come to those who wait." Often when waiting for something we want to happen we begin to lose patience with this sentiment. So many of us hold onto a dream for so long, and then give up in frustration before it can come to fruition. Remember that the best things in life are worth waiting for.

Planning for the Future

- Decide what you really want out of life. It's wise to consider if your dreams are practical, but don't give up before you even try. Once we evaluate our strengths we can work on attaining our dreams, one step at a time.

- We're here on this earth for a purpose, and that is to live the best life possible to realize the heights of our own individual potential. We all have a different path to lead, so don't measure your own life by the success of others.

- Life is all about the journey and what we learn along the way. Hitting our goals is the icing on the cake. Nothing worth obtaining comes easy, but having the tenacity to stick with something no matter how difficult will allow you to master it over time.

Visualizing Your Future Success

When you look at a mature tree you're

seeing years and years of steady growth and an example of nature's ability to thrive against all odds. When you hold an acorn in your hand, you're holding onto great potential, only attainable with the passage of time. While a tree can only manifest one future for itself, human potential is limitless. You can overcome adversity to succeed at whatever you want, as long as you stick to your plan and work hard.

★ CELEBRATION ★

Abundance

I trust in the universe to provide for me.
I am grateful for what I have.

Nature excels at providing for her children. In a balanced environment all creatures have access to what they need to thrive. Animals don't have to worry about how to get sustenance, as every leaf, fruit, seed, or berry is offered up freely to those who need. The circle of life is perfectly equipped to sustain all. In the fall, when the season begins to wind down, the foragers find ample supplies to store away, to keep them through the harsh winter. Nature in her infinite wisdom provides for her children in abundance, and they in turn enjoy a brief season of feasting before settling down for the long, cold months ahead.

Sometimes we get so caught up in materialism that we forget how rich our lives already are. You can't fill the hole in your heart with the things that you buy, and you can't appreciate how fortunate you really are if you are always craving more.

Appreciating What We Have

- Remember at least once a day to express gratitude to the Universe for providing for your needs. If there is food on the table, a roof over your head and clothes on your back, your life is already abundant. Cultivating gratitude sends a message to the Universe that you understand how fortunate you are. We attract the attention of the Universe with our thoughts, so invite continued abundance into your life by fostering an attitude of thankfulness.

- Next time you feel the urge for an impulse buy, ask yourself honestly why you feel the need. Are you simply bored, or maybe unhappy? Will this purchase improve your life in any appreciable way? While a frivolous purchase can be fun once in a while, it's important to take care of your needs first, before your wants.

- Cultivate generosity. Responding to others in need nurtures our own spirit while providing a better life for someone else. Once you truly understand how fortunate you are the pressure to amass possessions will begin to abate. Supporting another in their time of need will inspire them to pay it forward, creating a circle of generosity that will ripple outward to affect countless others. By cultivating generosity, we drive positive change in our society.

- Practice minimalism. Clutter creates an unhealthy atmosphere in our homes, so lighten and brighten things up with a good tidying. Keep only things that are useful, and that truly make you happy.

Experience Nature's Bounty

Planting a garden is a wonderful way to see firsthand how nature provides. If you don't have room for a garden, even a pot of herbs on your windowsill will do. It's a magical thing to eat something that you've grown yourself! Growing a garden provides us with the best possible nourishment for our bodies, and reconnects us with the earth. It gives us a sense of accomplishment and an appreciation for the simpler things in life. If you already have a garden and have the room, consider donating a row to a local food pantry, or share the harvest with a neighbor or friend.

Blossom

My life is full of amazing potential.
I am a beautiful flower about to blossom.

★ Blossom ★

Surely one of the most gorgeous outcomes of nature's diversity is the unfurling of a blossom. Flowers fill the wilderness with beautiful color, graceful form, and luxurious fragrance. Either singly on a branch, or in clusters that cover the forest floor, flowers are a delight to the eye and catch our attention with a quick glance. They herald the spring thaw and grace the summer months with beauty. They truly represent the pinnacle of nature's potential!

Each of us holds within ourselves at least one bud waiting to bloom. This is the genesis of our true calling or passion. It's the potential within waiting to express itself in our personal growth. The daily grind often replaces passion with practicality. Think of how much better the world would be if we all had the time and means to explore what's really meaningful to us! Who knows how many more brilliant poets, artists and great thinkers there would be if they'd been encouraged to blossom? As a society it should be our job to nurture and support the growth of talent and the creative arts!

Growing from Within

- Every single human no matter what their circumstances, has potential for growth. Have you ever told yourself you'd love to be able to do something, but lack the talent? Talent is the result of being interested enough in something to practice it consistently. Never let a perceived lack of talent hold you back from trying something new.

- Make a conscious effort to expand your horizons. Reading is one of the best ways to keep mentally sharp, spark imagination, and learn new things. Pick up a book from the library or search for video tutorials online. No matter what topic you're interested in, there is a tutorial for it.

- If you want to try something new but just aren't sure what, try shaking up your normal routine. Start a positivity journal, making note of interesting things you've seen during the day, or things you're grateful for, to help cultivate a happier mindset that's more receptive to change. Take note of things that draw your attention for clues to latent interests.

- Support the arts, for the good of yourself and your community. Buy from local artisans. Not only will that help them realize their dreams, you'll have something beautiful with a direct connection to the artist to enjoy. Spare some change when you pass by a busker. These very small gestures help others blossom, and will give you a sense of satisfaction.

Beautiful Inspiration

Of all nature's treasures, flowers are the most beautiful things that we have access to, and can easily be kept in a vase year-round. You can usually find them at your local grocer's. If you have a garden, plant for each season to provide year-round inspiration. Surrounding yourself with flowers delights the eye, and helps you cultivate your artistic side. They add beauty to a room and remind us of the potential we all have within.

★ Color ★

Color

I am happy and creative.
My life is colorful, joyful,
and inspired.

One of the first things we notice about any landscape is color. Limitless blue skies, crisp green fields, and pops of multi-hued flowers make us feel happy and inspired. Color truly has the ability to affect how we feel, and adds variety and beauty to our lives. In the wild, color is not only gorgeous, it also serves specific purposes. It can attract attention, like the brilliant hues of a peacock's tail. It can also hide, like the camouflage of a mottled moth's wing. Nature uses color to stand out, and also to blend in. It can signal maturity, like the ripeness of a juicy red apple, or danger, in the brilliant colors of a coral snake.

Color has the power to inspire us and to influence our moods. A pop of color in our wardrobe can make us feel happy and confident, while a simple grey suit can help us blend into a group. Different categories of colors can help us alter our moods, and send specific messages on a subconscious level.

Color Your Life With Inspiration

- Blues are cool, calming, and relaxing. Look up to a clear sunny sky and you'll feel a sense of peace spread over you. The color of heaven and ocean, blue represents serenity and peace so it's a good choice to paint a bedroom to promote sleep. Darker shades of blue are great to wear when you want to project a feeling of competence and seriousness.

- Reds are warm and energizing, and get noticed! In nature red is used to draw attention, and wearing red can help you stand out in a crowd. A pop of red in your decor can provide an exciting focal point. Red is associated with love, which is why red roses are a popular romantic gift. Wear red when you want to feel confident!

- Yellows and oranges are cheerfully energetic, and give us an optimistic feeling. Think of bright yellow sunshine, or the sweet savor of a perfectly ripened orange. Wear yellow and you'll be sure to project a happy vibe. Use pops of both colors around the home to impart a sunny and lively atmosphere.

- Many years ago purple was reserved for royalty so purple can evoke a feeling of luxury. Softer hues of lavender and mauve can feel romantic and feminine.

- Green is the color of life. What we see as green when we look at the forest is really a myriad of shades, creating a diverse blanket of color. Green is refreshing, yet calming because of the feeling of naturalness it evokes.

- Brown makes us feel grounded and brings a feeling of the outdoors into the home. Many natural materials we use for furnishings are brown. In decor and clothing it plays well with all other colors and can help tone them down.

- Black and white are statement colors. Black can represent darkness and evil for some, but also simplicity and sophistication. White often represents purity and morality. An all-white outfit certainly stands out, but can project an air of impracticality.

Color Your Life

Experimenting with color is as easy as setting up a vase of flowers. Try picking up a bouquet the next time you go shopping, and see how much it can uplift your mood. If you're in a more experimental frame of mind, try painting an accent wall in a bright color. You'd be amazed how much the right choice of color can brighten up your day!

Diversity

Diversity is beautiful and life affirming.

I celebrate, accept, and encourage diversity in others.

★ Diversity ★

Diversity is the building block of nature. The more complex an ecosystem, the healthier it is. The wider the variety of life, the better it functions, and the more resilient it becomes. The icing on the cake is that diversity in nature is beautiful. It allows creatures to evolve and adapt to take advantage of every niche available. Diversity celebrates life, and contributes to the health and well-being of all.

Just as complex environments encourage growth, health, and harmony, diverse cultures show us the potential for human innovation and evolution. Divergent ideas help us see problems from other angles, and give us insights we couldn't achieve on our own. Learning to accept and honor others because of their differences helps us grow along our spiritual path. Treating others with respect has the potential to create a harmonious life for all. Think of how much better life could be for everyone if we just practiced tolerance.

Learning from Others

- Cultivating an attitude of humility can be the first step toward acceptance of others. Some of us are too closed-minded to realize that our own thoughts and beliefs may be biased and flawed. Arrogance breeds intolerance, so stop thinking of your viewpoints as infallible.

- Acknowledge the possibility that others' ideas, habits, and lifestyles may be worthy of consideration. Just because someone else has a different viewpoint from ours, does not mean they are wrong. Embracing new ideas gives us a different perspective on the world.

- If you are ashamed to admit your own biases, please know this is a problem many of us share. To be human is to be flawed, so accept that you have room to improve and promise yourself to do better.
- Challenge yourself to learn about other cultures and lifestyles. Often prejudice is based in ignorance, which is combated with an open mind and education. Once you try to understand why others act and think the way they do, you can begin to see the value in the way they live.

Celebrate Diversity

There is no end to the examples of diversity in nature. Trees may all have leaves, but all leaves look different. Seashells provide homes for the creatures that build them, but each kind builds their shell to their own specification. Even no two snowflakes are alike! Look around you, and see how diverse nature really is, and how harmoniously these differences support each other for the good of all. Once you see how crucial diversity is in nature, begin to open your eyes to the potential of diversity in your own life. Educating yourself about other cultures dispels fear, one of the biggest drivers of intolerance. Imagine how stagnant human society would be without the wonderful mixture of ideas and new aesthetics that other cultures bring with them!

★ Freedom ★

Freedom

My physical body does not limit my experience of the cosmos.

My mind and spirit are free to grow, learn, and experience wonders.

In humanity's infancy, we were much more connected to the world around us, including the stars in the night sky. As we sat around our fires at night and looked up, we beheld those myriad sparkling lights and imagined them to be the campfires of our ancestors. In this way we felt a kinship with them, and didn't feel tethered to the earth permanently. We believed that after our time on earth was done, we'd rise to meet our ancestors and live in the sky in a glorious new life. While we knew that life could be hard, we truly understood that this existence couldn't contain us, and we had utter faith in the glories to come.

As the centuries moved along, humankind used curiosity and intelligence to develop new skills, new tools, and new ways of organizing ourselves. Civilization became more complex, and to a degree life because easier. While we understand more now, we believe in the miraculous less. When we focus on physical comforts, we forget the freedom of an expanded mind. We need to rediscover our connection with cosmos.

Let Your Spirit Fly

- Free yourself from the distractions of modern life that are meant to keep us placated but leave us unfulfilled. Don't fall into the trap of thinking what you can buy determines your self-worth. Once we begin to move away from a materialistic view of the word, we can begin to develop the spirituality we left behind with our ancestors.

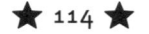

- Most of us are so grounded in our bodies we forget that our spiritual development is the real purpose for our existence. A simple mindful practice can help you move your focus beyond your body so you can begin to experience your spiritual side. A prayer of gratitude once a day is a good place to start. It's not necessary to thank a specific deity if you're not religious, but simply send a warm thought of appreciation out to the universe.

Connecting With the Cosmos

Sit comfortably is a quiet space, outside if at all possible. Close your eyes, and focus on your breath. Try to calm your mind. When you feel relaxed, try to feel the space within your skull. Feel the limits of this space and consider how our consciousness is contained within this area. Now begin to focus your attention outside your head. Expand your thoughts and try to feel the surroundings around you. With your eyes closed, it's easier to get a sense of all your surroundings. As that happens, try expanding your consciousness further out. While our physical bodies are tethered to our physical universe, our minds are free to wander as far as they want. Expanding our minds in this way helps remind us we're only earthbound for a brief moment in time.

Music

I raise my voice in song and join in the joyful celebration of life.

★ Music ★

Unscripted and inspired, nature's wild music greets us as we enter the forest. Dawn is celebrated by a chorus of birdsong, which settles into more languid notes as the heat of afternoon approaches. As the brightness of day dims and cools in the evening, more gentle sounds like the occasional hoot of an owl and the chirping of crickets and frogs are heard. No matter what the time or season, nature abounds with the happy music of creatures celebrating their very existence. In nature, music is multipurpose. It proclaims joy and signals intent. It's communication in its purest form, as nuanced and complex as human speech.

Humanity has always striven to create its own music. From the very dawn of time we have embraced music as entertainment, communication and worship. Music is ubiquitous today and fills our lives from wake to sleep, from the alarm clock that starts our day with our favorite radio station, to the music that helps us relax at night. Musicians are among the most admired artists, inspiring many of us to create our own music. Remember how all of us as children broke into uninhibited song simply for the joy of it. Singing or playing music is a very pure way of practicing mindfulness, and it's within all of our abilities to learn how.

Healing With Music

- Having a musical practice can be a form of mindfulness meditation. Learning to play an instrument forces us to focus on what we are doing, and helps us disconnect temporarily from the distractions around us. As you do an activity you enjoy, it calms the mind and leaves you feeling refreshed.

- Music has a strong power to evoke moods and memories. For most people important moments in their lives are inextricably tied with a particular song. Happy songs are an instant mood elevator, while sad songs can help us get through a tough patch like a relationship breakup. If you're feeling particularly blue, try listening to some upbeat music and see how much better you feel afterwards.

- Keep an open mind, and try new genres. It's great to hold onto old favorite songs, but there's always room to add new music to your playlist. These days music is so accessible there's no reason not to experiment!

- Make your own music! Try singing out loud, or even dancing to your favorite tune. Singing is good exercise. It works your heart and lungs and oxygenates the blood, which will help lift your mood. This body-mind stimulation promotes physical as well as mental well-being.

Listening to Nature

The next time you're outside, perk up your ears and take note of the sounds around you. Listen to the birds cheerfully calling and pay attention to subtle sounds like the gentle susurration of leaves blowing in the wind. If you're out at night, listen for crickets, frogs, or cicadas chirping in the darkness. Notice how these sounds make you feel. As we pay attention to the music of nature, we begin to feel the bond it forms between us and the natural world. That sense of belonging and kinship with the world can help us feel less isolated, and more in tune with the natural order of things. It reminds us that we're just like all other living things, and that knowledge will help us feel more connected with the world around us.

Passion

Nothing will hold me back from enjoying life to the utmost.

★ Passion ★

Ah, spring! A riotous time of activity in the wild. The days grow warmer, milder, and fairly burst with the potential for new life. Animals scramble to attract a mate, and the amorous calls of birds fill the air. It's a time of reckless abandon and pure joy! Passion drives all living things to manifest the expression of life to the fullest. Passion is living in the moment, and allowing yourself to fully feel the joy of experiencing something you love.

Daily obligations can make us feel less passionate about our lives. While all of us need a little structure in our lives, too much becomes overwhelming and we no longer remember the sense of possibility life once had. If you have forgotten what it feels like to be really excited about something, it's time to rediscover your passion for life.

Finding Your Passion

- Try to do one spontaneous thing every day. Shaking up our routine can help us see our lives in a new light. While for the majority of us our obligations limit how much we can stray from our daily commitments, we can all do something new or different every day. Remember, every step away from the usual has the potential to open up infinite possibilities for our future.

- Practice mindfulness. Our multitasking society trains our brains to partially focus on many things at once, so a lot of us find it hard to focus on one thing at a time. You can't enjoy one thing fully if your attention is fractured by a distracted mind.

- Remember, there is no limit to what we as individuals can do when we set our minds to it. No matter what you're interested in, you have the capability of learning and even excelling at it.

- If, like many people, you're really not sure what you're passionate about, think hard about the things that make you happy, and work from there. Do you like working with your hands? Maybe it's time to stop thinking of your hobbies as pleasant pastimes, and instead as a possible career path. You never know what sort of exciting possibilities will open up when you follow your passions.

Let Nature Jumpstart Your Passion

Nature helps evoke feelings of awe and wonderment, which reminds us of what life's potential can really mean for us. It's impossible not to feel moved by a particularly lovely sunrise. The burgeoning rosy color in the sky and the gentle bird calls that rise to greet the sun give us a sense of optimism and hope. The fresh, clean feeling in the air after a rainfall clears our minds and leaves us feeling invigorated. Being in nature reminds us how simply lovely life can feel. Let nature inspire you, then use that inspiration to spark passion in your life and relationships.

Summer

Every day has potential for joy. Today I choose to be happy.

★ Summer ★

Summer is truly the happiest time of year. It is the time when all living creatures can pause and enjoy life to the utmost. Animal babies grow and play, while their parents relax before the busy preparations for winter begin. Food is plentiful, and the evenings are languid and friendly. Summer is a time of rest and rejuvenation, a time for warmth and healing.

Sometimes, as adults we need to be reminded to slow down once in a while, and allow ourselves time to enjoy life. When we do take time to rest, often we feel guilty and don't enjoy it as much as we should. There's always so much to be done! While our lives may be comfortable and secure, how many of us experience true joy, especially day to day? If we have forgotten how to play, we need to reignite the spark of childhood whimsy, that magical way of looking at the world that sees the potential of fun in everything.

Becoming Happier

- Give yourself permission to have fun. A lot of people get anxious when they're taking time to do something they enjoy. We work to live; we don't live to work. Taking a moment for yourself out of a busy day isn't being lazy; it's essential to your long-term well-being. Allow yourself to have fun once in a while.

- Cultivate gratitude. Many of us are unhappy because we're working to achieve a standard of material possessions that is unrealistic. We forget to be grateful for all the blessings we already have. There is no hole to fill in your life if you're grateful for what you have.

- Learn to say no, and don't let yourself drown in unnecessary obligations. Your downtime is as important as everyone else's; so don't take on other people's burdens. Designate chores if you need to, instead of picking up the slack for others. Don't make yourself available to others all the time. It's good to turn your phone off once in a while. The world will get by without you for a time.

- Let go of inhibitions. Don't spend a moment worrying about what other people might think, as this gives them power over your happiness. Want to go dancing but are scared of looking foolish? Then dance like no one's looking! Often we fear being judged so much that it prevents us from doing things we enjoy. If someone judges you for superficial reasons, that is all about where they are on their path, and has nothing to do with you.

Have Fun!

Taking a nature break is an amazing and effective way of connecting with our inner child. Climb a tree, balance along a log, or jump over puddles. Find a place where there aren't any people around and simply play! Skip some stones over a lake, whistle back at the birds, and make sure to talk to any animals you happen to see, and thank them for visiting you! Have a little fun in private, and it will remind your spirit of how childhood felt. This will carry over into your adult life over time. If climbing trees or jumping over rocks isn't your thing, simply enjoy the beauty around you. Feel how good the warm sun is on your face, and how refreshing the breeze is. How good it is to be comfortable and surrounded by beauty. This is true happiness!

Whimsy

I will stop taking myself so seriously and find joy in the frivolities of life.

★ Whimsy ★

Life in the wild is not always serious business. Observe animals and you'll see that even full grown, they don't forget how to play! If you've ever owned a cat you will have seen no matter their age they never lose the urge to be silly once in a while. Even the most reluctant wild mother can't resist joining in the fun when her little ones beckon. Play for young animals helps them develop skills they'll need when they're all grown up, which is true of human children as well. It helps us see the world creatively and teaches us to think outside the box. Childhood imagination allowed us to see life as wonderful and exciting, full of adventure and new experiences just around the bend. It let us explore all the possibilities the world had to offer in a safe and creative way.

Reawaken Your Inner Child

- Allow yourself to enjoy frivolous diversions. As adults we sometimes feel we must act with seriousness and productivity at all times, and the burden of responsibilities weighs heavy on us. This sense of obligation can make us feel guilty when we take time away from work. If necessary, schedule leisure time every day.

- Don't feel it's necessary to act like an adult all the time. Caring too much about what others think of us can dampen any enthusiasm in having fun, so stop worrying about looking silly and enjoy yourself!

- Life's too short to be serious all the time, so enjoy the little things that spark joy. Who says adults can't wear cute shirts, or socks with kitties on them? Why not hang a fun and colorful poster on your wall, or make a batch of rainbow cookies? Remember that the standards that society assigns to grownups are arbitrary and there's no reason to let these random expectations spoil your fun.

- Use your imagination, and try to look at the world through the eyes of a child again. We once saw the world around us as a magical place full of endless possibilities, and it's possible to regain a little of that childish outlook. Greet each day as an exciting opportunity to see or experience something new, and go out of your way to do things on a whim. We never lose our capacity for imagination; it's just waiting for us to start using it again.

- Cultivate your sense of wonder. When we were kids life was amazing! Just because we now understand the science behind things like a lightning bolt or a rainbow doesn't make them any less miraculous. Who says the world reflected in a puddle isn't a portal to another reality? Remember to look for castles in the clouds and view the world as more than just what meets the eye.

Making Rainbows

For a bit of whimsy on a warm day, head outside, sit on the grass, and blow soap bubbles. There are all kinds of recipes you can find online for making bubble soap, but a basic mixture is one part dish soap to two parts water. Make a circle on the end of a twist tie, and blow to your heart's content! Watch the bubbles float away on the breeze, and feel your tension floating away with every shimmering rainbow-coated sphere. Feel how happy it makes you to do something so simple and fun!

Wild

I will not allow social convention to define me.
I will follow my heart along unconventional paths to find my authentic self.

★ Wild ★

How unconventional is your life? Is it exciting and motivating, or regimented and boring? Do you forge your own path, or play by the rules? While most of us are pretty content with our day-to-day routine, sometimes we get bored and feel uninspired. We do what we have to do to get by, and get buried under obligations. If you're feeling trapped, it's time to break free of routines.

The wild creatures that live out their lives in freedom do best without the taming hand of man. As humans we often seek to control everything around us. We suppress natural urges, and impart a rigid structure to our societies. In our hearts we're still wild and independent, but we've just been taught our whole lives to live up to society's expectations. The tiniest mouse in the field is freer that some of us will ever be. It doesn't worry about living its life according to someone else's ideal. It simply is.

Seeking Independence

- If you're not ready to take the plunge into a new career due to financial constraints, there's nothing stopping you from exploring the possibilities out there. Don't settle for a job that makes you miserable because it's the safest option. Often exploration can start as hobbies, and hobbies can lead to finding your passion, which opens the door of possibility in your life.

- Spend some time in solitude once in a while, to give yourselves time to think. If you're surrounded by others all the time it's hard to focus exclusively on yourself. Remember, you're not required to be available to family or friends at all times. Hire a babysitter, go for a walk by yourself, or learn to say no when asked to do something you're not enthusiastic about. Remember to prioritize your own needs. It's hard to remember who we really are when we define our value in life by service to others.

- Remember, it's never too late to find your passion. As humans we're adaptable and always capable of learning. Don't let another day go by without trying something new you've always wanted to do. No need to plunge into the deep end—exploring your options can be as simple as reading a book. And don't let age be an excuse when you're afraid to try something new. Who says we have to live by standards society deems age appropriate? Push the boundaries that others have placed on you. Life's too short to play it safe!

Take a Walk on the Wild Side

Spending time outside at night is a great way to reconnect to your wild side. Experiencing the dark and speculating on what it can conceal can be exhilarating, but make sure you're in a safe place like your backyard. Ideally you should lie on the grass, but if that's not possible pull up a lawn chair, or simply stand in a comfortable spot. Note how the darkness conceals and makes the world around us seem mysterious and exciting. Imagine how it would feel to simply melt into the darkness, and become one with the creatures who move just outside the limits of our vision. Look up at the stars, and feel how wonderful it is not to be boxed in by walls. The night is alive with possibilities. The whole world is out there for you to explore. All it takes is one brave step.

BONUS CARD

Contentment

I am perfectly happy with my life.

My gratitude and patience manifests perfect contentment.

In nature when it's storming, there's nothing to do but wait it out. Activity stops, and all the creatures of the forest find a cozy spot to patiently watch the rain fall. Watching the raindrops from their sheltered space, they patiently wait, using their idle time to rest and simply be. They know nothing can rush the forces of nature, and they trust in the promise of clear skies to follow. Storms come, and storms go, but life continues without fail.

Contentment is what we experience when we practice patience and gratitude in our lives. Patience is the ability to set aside anger and frustration while waiting for things to change. Gratitude is an expression of appreciation for all the Universe has given us. When we are grateful for what we have it allows us to deal with setbacks without becoming stressed and upset. We know that the Universe is working to manifest bounty in our lives, and we're willing to wait for it. We don't allow adversity to take our minds off the many blessings we enjoy. Gratitude is how we show the Creator that we appreciate what we've been given, and contentment is the feeling we get when we know all in our lives is how it should be.

Taming Impatience

- As humans we like to tell ourselves that we are capable of controlling all aspects of our lives. The fact is, in the grand scheme of things, we're part of a bigger picture than we're able to see. When we experience setbacks and adversity we're upset that things are not going as we expect them. We can't see the reasons behind the way things happen as they do. At such times it's comforting to think that all that happens to us serves a greater purpose.

- When anticipating something good we're often impatient, willing the time to go faster so we can experience that good thing as soon as possible. Often when we do attain it it's over so fast the pleasure is fleeting. Appreciating the fact that something anticipated is still in our futures can help us learn to be patient.

- Practicing gratitude grounds us in the here and now, and helps us appreciate our lives as they are. There are always reasons to be grateful, no matter what hardships you're going through. Take time to appreciate what you do have, instead of stressing about what you don't. When we are truly grateful for what we have in our lives, we won't want to hurry time along. We'll take our time to truly appreciate our time here, and not diminish our experience of life by wishing the present away.

An Attitude of Gratitude

A regular practice of gratitude is the bedrock of a life of contentment. It keeps us from despair when times are tough, and allows us to be patient when awaiting something positive. Our time on earth is meant to be a time of spiritual growth, and the Universe sends us the lessons we need to learn and grow. None of us are guaranteed a life where everything is perfect, but all of us can be happy and content with our own lives. Next time it rains, make a nice cup of tea, and sit down to watch the storm. Think about all the birds, insects, and animals sitting patiently in their nooks and crannies, waiting for the rain to end. Allow this patience to enter your own heart. Sip your tea, enjoy your rest, and be thankful for your warm cozy home that allows you to wait the storm out in comfort and security.

About the Artist and Author

From my earliest memories of childhood I have been a prolific artist, and an avid reader with an endless imagination. When not wandering the lands of Middle Earth or Narnia, I could be found traipsing through the woods on my own, as wild in my mind as the rabbits in the underbrush. I was blessed with a mother who inspired me to create with my hands, a father who passed on his love of nature to me, and an older brother who sparked my voracious appetite for reading.

The world of fiction exposed me to many different philosophies and cultures at an early age, sparking a life-long fascination with the exotic and sublime diversity of life. My love of nature keeps me grounded, and I enjoy creating art that is positive and life-affirming. If I put a smile on your face I feel my job is well done! I find pleasure in the small things in life—a good cup of tea, a walk in the woods, or the sound of rain falling on the roof. I hope when you view my work it lifts your spirits and helps you feel the potential for joy that every day brings. To see more of my artwork, please visit me on Facebook at Bliss and Kittens and on Instagram @BlissAndKittens.

I wish you love, light, and happiness in all you do.

~ Brenda Saydak

Notes

Notes

For our complete line of tarot decks, books, meditation and yoga cards, oracle sets, and other inspirational products please visit our website:
www.usgamesinc.com

Follow us on:

f **t** **p** **O**

U.S. GAMES SYSTEMS, INC.
179 Ludlow Street
Stamford, CT 06902 USA
Phone: 203-353-8400
Order Desk: 800-544-2637
FAX: 203-353-8431